# 3-D THRILLERS!

# PREHISTORIC WORLD

PAUL HARRISON

Capella

**I**f you had the chance to see the world about 4.5 billion years ago when it first came into being you could not have imagined it would ever look the way it does now. Back then it was little more than a ball of molten rock. Eventually it cooled, rains fell and seas formed, but the earth was surrounded in poisonous gasses. Not an enticing prospect.

## THE BEGINNING

The first living things on earth were not impressive to look at. In fact they were microscopic bacteria, so your chances of seeing them with the naked eye would be zilch. The bacteria and microbes which first appeared on earth produced oxygen, the gas most life needs to breathe. Some bacteria formed colonies which, over time, built into stromatolites. There are fossils of these things which are over 3 billion years old!

You can still see stromatolites today. Hamelin Pool in Western Australia is one famous sight where these ancient structures can be found.

## WATERY WONDERS

The early oceans were the place to be if you were looking for life. After bacteria came simple animals such as sponges and jellyfish. However one of the early success stories was the trilobites. They look a bit like underwater woodlice, which isn't really surprising as they're related. Trilobites ruled the oceans for nearly 300 million years despite the biggest of them only measuring in at around 70 cm. However all good things must come to an end and trilobites vanished from the seas about 250 million years ago.

# BEGINNING

## LATE DEVELOPER

The first fish made an appearance over 500 million years ago, but they were quite small and their mouths were always open because they didn't have jaws! Things changed quite a bit over the next 100 million years. By then, *Dunkleosteus* (dunk-lee-OWE-stee-us), a chunky, 10 metre long super-predator was terrorizing the seas. Around this time the first sharks appeared, too, so it was quite a dangerous place to be for any lunch-sized sea creatures.

## NOT SO FUNNY

The earliest predators were a strange-looking bunch. Take *Anomalocaris* (a-nom-uh-lo-CARE-is) for example; it was the scourge of the seas over 500 million years ago. It looked like a large shrimp with a trunk-like arms next to its mouth for catching prey. Or there's *Eurypterids* (you-RIP-ter-ids)– which looked like a bug-eyed monster. They might have looked odd, but they were good at one thing in particular, catching prey; and when you're a predator that's all that counts.

# ON LAND

**T**he survival instinct is one of the reasons animals evolve, so if all the other animals are in the sea the next place to try to live is on land — handy for escaping from all those predators.

## IT'S A MYSTERY

Scientists aren't sure exactly what the first animal to venture onto land was. We do know that it must have been able to breathe air as well as in the water. Scientists think that fish first developed the ability to take breaths of air, and may have been able to pull themselves out of the water. Some people believe an animal called *Pederpes* (peh-DER-pees) was the first creature to be able to actually walk on the land. It lived around 350 million years ago and there have been creatures on land ever since.

## PLANTS POP UP

The first plants appeared over 400 million years ago. They were hugely important as plants changed the make-up of the atmosphere. One of the most widely-known was cooksonia. It wasn't much of a plant as it was small and didn't have any leaves or flowers; but it was a start. Over the next few million years plants evolved from these humble origins to huge forests.

## BIG INSECTS

Once the land had been conquered the next place was the air. Insects were the first to get there, though it took them a while – about 70 million years to be exact as the first insects couldn't fly. Once they had evolved around 330 million years ago, they made up for lost time with some of the most impressive insects ever seen – some dragonflies had wingspans up to 70 cm across! Imagine that buzzing around your ice cream.

**An animal that can breathe both on land and in water is called an amphibian.**

## FINTASTIC

Around 70 million years after animals first left the water the reptiles evolved. Originally they were quite small but soon developed into more formidable creatures. One of the most ferocious was *Dimetrodon* (di-MET-ro-don) who stalked the earth around 270 million years ago. One of its more noticeable features was the bony fin on its back. Scientists think this might have helped Dimetrodon to warm up. As a reptile it would be cold-blooded which means it would have relied on the sun's warmth to get it going. Dimetrodon might have been an awesome proposition, but compared to the reptiles that appeared a few million years later it was a lightweight.

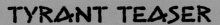

**A** round 200 million years ago the world was governed by some of the most famous animals ever — the dinosaurs. Their reign lasted for over 165 million years — but you could argue that it continues today, because dinosaurs are the distant but direct relatives of birds.

## TYRANT TEASER

The most famous dinosaur of all is, of course, the fearsome *Tyrannosaurus rex* (tie-RAN-oh-SORE-us REX). Its name means "tyrant lizard king". Its razor sharp teeth were the size of bananas and its powerful jaws could smash through thick bones; but some scientists claim it was too slow to chase other dinosaurs and ate animals that were already dead. Others claim that T. rex was a classic ambush predator. Either way, it wouldn't be advisable to laugh at those funny little arms.

## BIGGEST OF ALL?

We all know that some dinosaurs were big, but we're not sure exactly which one was the biggest of all. Current favourites to take the record include *Argentinosaurus* (ar-gen-TEEN-o-SORE-us) and *Seismosaurus* (size-moh-SORE-us). At lengths of up to 35 metres (115 feet) and weighing in at over 60 000 kilogrammes (66 tons), these giants could peer over the top of a house – though they might leave some nasty footprints in the flower beds.

New dinosaur species are being discovered all the time. Around 40% of all known dinosaurs were found in the last twenty years.

## WINGED WONDERS

Dinosaurs were not only reptiles to roam the earth at this time. There were others too, such as the flying pterosaurs. They had leathery wings, a bit like a bat's, and could, scientists believe, glide and soar through the air. The largest was Quetzalcoatlus, with a wing span of around 12 metres (40 feet), but not all pterosaurs were this big – some were no bigger than a small bird.

## SMALL AND FEATHERY

Not all dinosaurs were earth-shaking giants. A lot of them were small, scurrying creatures no bigger than chickens. It's hard to say which dinosaur is the smallest – partly because so little evidence of some species remains to be sure they are adults or just young dinosaurs. However many scientists believe that small dinosaurs, such as *Caudipteryx* (caw-DIP-ter-iks), were covered in feathers to help keep them warm.

T he dinosaurs disappeared in somewhat mysterious circumstances around 65 million years ago. No one quite knows why – all we do know is that over 50% of all life was wiped out. This was bad news for dinosaurs but great news for mammals.

## A WHAT?

A mammal is warm-blooded which means it generates its own body heat – unlike a reptile – and gives birth to live young. The first mammals actually shared the planet with the dinosaurs. In those days many mammals were quite small, about the size of a rat. However, recent finds suggest that some mammals grew a bit bigger – over a metre in fact – and some even ate other dinosaurs!

## MONKEYING AROUND

When the dinosaurs died out, the lack of competition gave the mammals room to grow and diversify. Around 60 million years ago the first primates – apes and monkeys – evolved. The most complete remains found so far belong to *Proconsul africanus* (pro-CON-sul Afri-KHAN-us) which lived around 18 million years ago. It walked on four legs and probably ate fruit. I wonder if there were bananas back then?

# MAMMALS

### GIDDY UP

The first horses appeared over 40 million years ago. One of the most famous is *Hyracotherium* (high-rah-co-THEER-ium) often called *Eohippus* (ee-oh-HIP-us) or the "dawn horse". It didn't look much like a horse; for a start it didn't have hooves but had toes instead, much like a dog's foot. The similarities don't end there; Hyracotherium was only 20cm high. It's safe to say you wouldn't be jumping many fences if you rode one of those!

There is a third type of mammal known as monotremes – these are mammals which lay eggs!

### MARSUPIALS

Marsupials are mammals which carry their new-born young in a pouch where they continue to develop; the most famous modern-day marsupials are kangaroos. In the past marsupials were much more common then they are now. The first ones rubbed shoulders with dinosaurs and later they diverged into all shapes and sizes. There were carnivores, too, such as *Sparassodonta patene* (spar-ASS-oh-don-ta Pah-ten), a fox-sized predator from Brazil. No doubt it was a bit fiercer than a koala.

# UNDER

**W**hile on land the dinosaurs appeared then disappeared again, below the waves there was a lot going on too. Life in the water was expanding and diversifying, producing all sorts of interesting creatures.

## BIG FISH

At just under 30 metres long *Leedsichthys* (leeds-ICK-thees) was not only the biggest fish of its time, it was the biggest fish of all time – imagine how many chips you would need with that! It may seem odd, but Leedsichthys wasn't a mean old predator; this huge fish ate tiny sea creatures called plankton, which was good news for all the other fish!

## SHELL-SHOCK

Turtles have been around for over 100 million years and some of them were huge. *Archelon* (ARK-eh-lon) lived alongside the dinosaurs and died out at the same time. Apart from its size – it was about as big as a car – it had other differences with today's turtles. The main one was its shell, which wasn't hard but leathery – which left it vulnerable to attack. Not much point having a shell if it's soft, is there?

# WATER

## BIG SNAPPER

A lot of the animals we know today had relatives who lived millions of years ago. This is true of crocodiles, whose ancestors not only knew dinosaurs, but possibly ate them, too. *Sarcosuchus* (sar-co-SOOK-us), which lived over 100 million years ago, was certainly big enough to snap up an unwary dinosaur. It was around 12 metres long and had jaws were long enough to swallow your teacher whole. It's a pity you can't get one from a pet shop – one quick bite and no more maths!

## BACK TO THE SEA

After waiting for so long for creatures to come out of the water and onto the land, it seems odd that some went in the opposite direction; but that's exactly what whales did. They evolved from land mammals that began to spend increasing amounts of time in the water until eventually their legs turned into flippers. The first creature that looked like a modern whale was *Basilosaurus* (bah-sil-oh-SAW-rus) which lived around 45 million years ago. If it knew the problems its descendants would have today it might have wished it stayed on land.

**Leedsichthys was alive at the same time as the dinosaurs. It was swimming in the seas around 160 million years ago.**

# RISE OF THE

O n land the mammals faced no great competition and, like the dinosaurs before them, grew and evolved into a whole range of different shapes and sizes.

## BIGGEST OF ALL

If you think mammals such as elephants are big, you ain't seen nothing yet! The *Indricotherium* (IN-drik-oh-theer-um) was the biggest mammal to ever walk the earth. It lived over 25 million years ago and was around 4 metres tall. Fortunately for everything else that lived at the time, Indricotherium ate plants not meat. In fact the Indricotherium is a distant relative of today's rhinoceros. I wonder if the indricotherium was as grumpy and short-sighted as today's rhinos are?

## DANGEROUS GROUND

There are sloths alive today, but we know them as slow-moving creatures that spend the majority of their lives asleep in the trees. However, once there were sloths that lived on the ground and some of them were huge! When *Megatherium* (meg-ah-THEER-ee-um) stood on its back legs it was about 3 metres tall. As formidable as it was, Megatherium did die out, so maybe hiding in the trees was a better idea after all.

# MAMMALS

Many prehistoric mammal remains have been found in tar pits in California where the unfortunate animals got stuck in the tar and died.

## SURPRISINGLY SMALL

Not all the ancient mammals were giants of course; in fact some of the were smaller versions of animals that we know today. For example there was a species of dwarf elephant that lived as recently as around 8,000 years ago. They often lived on islands and some of were less than a metre tall. Despite their size, they still had relatively large ears, a trunk and tusks.

## BAD KITTY

There were some pretty mean mammalian carnivores around, and like today some of the most impressive were cat-like. *Thylacosmilus* (thy-la-COS-mih-lus) was a marsupial that lived in South America and was about the size of a jaguar. Its most striking feature was its two huge fangs. Safe to say that this was one cat you wouldn't want as a pet, but amazingly, this fearsome character was outdone by even bigger and meaner sabre-toothed cats.

# EARLY

**T**he whole human history story is mightily confused. For a start there's no clear picture of exactly how we developed. What might surprise you was there were many different types of early human, all of which died out apart from our own particular species. Meet the ancestors.

## HE OR SHE?

The oldest human remains found come from Africa and are nearly 6 million years old. Back then humans looked a lot like apes and even spent a good bit of their time in trees. One of the most famous discoveries is of a species known as *Australopithecus afarensis* (ostra-lo-PITH-ikus A-fa-REN-sis). The people who found the remains nicknamed them "Lucy" because they thought they were the bones of a female. However some scientists think "she" might have actually been a "he". Girl or boy, Lucy is over 3 million years old and stood about 1m high.

## FAMILY FEUD

There was also another highly successful species of human around – the Neanderthals. Shorter and heavier than *Homo sapiens* (HOE-mo SAY-pee-uns), they had been around for much longer – from around 150,000 years earlier. Neanderthals were thought to be more primitive than Homo sapiens; however some scientists now believe that they too were capable of doing art as well as hunt. Whatever the truth, the Neanderthals finally disappeared around 30,000 years ago, outperformed by their cousins the Homo sapiens.

# HUMANS

## ARTISTS

Our own direct relatives – Homo sapiens – have been around for at least 130,000 years. What made us different was our ability to think. Being a bit brainier meant that Homo sapiens could plan and work together better, leaving time to indulge in such exciting pastimes as cave art – it would be a long time before we invented television. Being clever also made us adaptable; and if you can adapt you can survive – and that's just what we did.

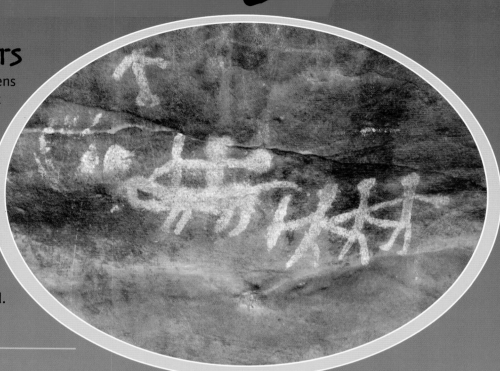

Our human ancestors and near relatives are known as 'hominids'.

## NO BRAINER

Recently a small skeleton was found on the Indonesian island of Flores. About 12,000 years old, the skeleton appeared to have a smaller brain than homo sapiens. About 1 metre tall it got nicknamed the Flores Hobbit. Scientists thought they had found a new species of human being. Now however many believe that they are the remains of a small homo sapien with a disease that made its brain smaller. It just goes to show how difficult this looking at the past can be.

This edition published in 2007 by Arcturus Publishing Limited
26/27 Bickels Yard, 151–153 Bermondsey Street,
London SE1 3HA

Copyright © 2007 Arcturus Publishing Limited

Author: Paul Harrison
Design: Top Floor Design Ltd.
Editor: Fiona Ball

Picture credits:
Corbis: page 3, bottom; page 8, bottom; page 11, top; page 11, bottom.
Getty: page 5, bottom.
Science Photo Library: title page; page 2; page 3, top; page 6, top and bottom; page 7; page 8; page 9, top; page 10, bottom; page 12, middle and bottom; page 13, top right; page 14, left and right; page 15, bottom; page 16.

3-D images by Pinsharp 3D Graphics

Printed in China

ISBN: 978-1-84193-660-4